CHARON NORMAND-WIDMER

Sovereign in Love

The Nervous System Path to Desire, Power and Intimacy

First published by Charon Normand-Widmer 2026

Copyright © 2026 by Charon Normand-Widmer

All rights reserved. No part of this publication may be reproduced, stored, or transmitted in any form or by any means, electronic, mechanical, photocopying, recording, scanning, or otherwise without written permission from the publisher. It is illegal to copy this book, post it to a website, or distribute it by any other means without permission.

For permission requests, write to the author at:
holisticharon.com

The information contained in this book is for educational purposes only. It is not intended as a substitute for professional therapeutic, medical, or psychological care. If you are experiencing a mental health crisis or require clinical support, please seek assistance from a qualified professional.

Printed in the United States of America

First edition

ISBN: 979-8-9953041-0-4

Editing by Jude Raphael Cabato

This book was professionally typeset on Reedsy.
Find out more at reedsy.com

For my husband: whose support never wavered and whose laughter made the journey lighter.

For my children: beautiful, patient, and generous beyond what I deserved.

For my family, my mentors, and my teachers: who shared their love and their work with me and trusted me to carry it forward.

For my clients: who received what moves through me and showed me it was real.

And for you, the reader: for the time you are giving these words and the courage it takes to want more for yourself.

Contents

Foreword

This book was not written from a distance.

It was written from two decades of sitting with people in the most vulnerable territory of their lives: in the aftermath of betrayal, in the confusion of desire, in the long and disorienting work of learning to feel safe in a body that learned early that safety was not guaranteed.

I am a somatic trauma practitioner, a relationship and intimacy coach, and I am a student of neuropsychoanalysis. I work at the intersection of nervous system science, erotic embodiment, and relational repair. I have sat with individuals and couples navigating the gap between who they understand themselves to be and how they actually show up when the heat rises and the body takes over.

That gap is what this book is about.

The framework you will find in these pages draws on polyvagal theory, predictive processing, somatic practice, and shadow work, but it is not a clinical text. It does not ask you to pathologize yourself or your history. It asks something simpler and more demanding: that you bring your body into the conversation about love.

Most books about relationships speak to the mind. They offer frameworks, communication tools, attachment maps. These things have value.

The nervous system does not reorganize through understanding. It reorganizes through experience, through the slow, repetitive, embodied practice of learning that what once felt dangerous is safe now.

That is what Sovereign in Love is designed to support.

The concepts here are grounded in neuroscience. The practices are grounded in the body. But the truth underneath all of it is simpler than any framework I could offer:

You cannot build a love that is steadier than you are.

And you are capable of becoming much steadier than you know.

I wrote this book because I needed it. Because the people I work with needed it. Because the particular conversation it is trying to start about nervous system capacity, erotic maturity, and the shadow of sovereignty, was not happening anywhere I could find it in the language it deserved.

If it meets you where you are, I am glad.

If it challenges you, I am glad of that too.

The body knows the difference between what is comfortable and what is true.

Trust the one that is true.

With care,

Charon holisticharon.com

Preface

This book uses the language of masculine and feminine energy throughout.

This language is not intended to map onto gender identity, biological sex, or relationship structure. It is used as shorthand for two complementary energetic orientations. directed and receptive, that exist within every person regardless of how they identify.

Where gendered language appears, it is in service of naming patterns that are culturally common, not universally fixed. The deeper invitation of this book belongs to everyone.

1

Chapter One

Stop Outsourcing Your Internal State

He hasn't texted back.

It's been three hours.

You tell yourself you're fine.

You are not fine.

Your chest is tight. Your stomach is hollow. Your thoughts are looping.

You open your phone. Close it. Open it.

You replay the last conversation.

Did I say too much? Was I too distant? Was I too available?

Your body is already negotiating a future that hasn't happened. You feel the faint edge of humiliation. The pull to send something casual. The urge to regain control.

It's not about the text.

It's about what your nervous system believes silence means.

Most people believe their lives would change if one thing outside them shifted.

You do not react to reality.

You react to expectations.

And expectation is memory. Memory lives in tissue.

Most people believe their lives would change if one external variable shifted. Suppose the partner showed up differently if the relationship felt safer. If the money increased. If the recognition came.

They imagine the circumstance will create the feeling.

But circumstances only stimulate. Your nervous system decides what they mean.

You do not feel desired because someone wants you. You feel desired because your body can relax into being wanted. You do not feel powerful because you succeed. You feel powerful because your system remains steady as it expands.

You do not feel secure because someone stays. You feel secure because your body no longer anticipates being left.

External events trigger. Internal states interpret. And interpretation happens before thought.

This is the fracture beneath most dissatisfaction: you are trying to change your life without changing your internal experience of yourself.

So you collect better conditions, and remain the same. The relationship improves; insecurity remains. The commitment deepens; vigilance remains. The love becomes undeniable; the bracing continues. The income increases; anxiety remains.

Because the nervous system does not reorganize when circumstances improve, it reorganizes when it feels safe.

You are not reacting to what is happening. You are reacting to what your body expects to happen. And the body moves fast.

You can intellectually know someone loves you, and still brace when they go quiet. You can intellectually know you are successful, and still feel like you're behind. You can intellectually know you are wanted, and still tighten when someone looks at you too long. Because your system is not responding to facts, it is responding to imprint.

Sovereignty begins here.

Not with confidence.

Not with standards.

Not with attraction.

With regulation.

Sovereignty is the ability to feel contraction, and not chase. To feel distance, and not collapse. To feel desire and not lose yourself in it. To feel someone's attention on your skin and stay present inside your own body. It is internal coherence. And coherence is magnetic.

Most people try to change the world to soothe their nervous system. Few regulate their nervous system to transform their world. So partners become regulators. Silence becomes a threat. Praise becomes oxygen. Withdrawal becomes annihilation. Desire becomes unstable because you are asking something outside of you to stabilize something inside of you.

No one can carry that.

This is not independence. It is internal leadership.

When someone withdraws, you feel it and remain steady. When someone disappoints you, you feel the sting and stay intact. When someone wants you, you feel the heat and do not grip. When conflict rises, you breathe instead of perform.

That is power. Not the absence of feeling, but stability within it.

You cannot build sovereign love while outsourcing your nervous system. You cannot sustain polarity while collapsing under fluctuation. You cannot experience grounded intimacy if your internal state fractures every time connection shifts.

Before attraction. Before communication. Before devotion.
There is regulation.
This is where we begin.

2

Chapter Two

The Speed of Imprint

You said you would not react like that again. You promised yourself. You have insight, you understand your patterns.

You have read the books.

You have done the therapy.

Then, they pulled away.

Only slightly. Their tone shifted. Their eye contact thinned. Their response time stretched longer than usual. Your body decided before your mind arrived.

Your chest tightened.

Your stomach dropped.

Your jaw locked.

Colder. Sharper. Quieter.

The reaction was immediate. It felt justified. Identity stepped in afterward to explain it. Your nervous system had already acted. Most people believe they are responding to what is happening. They are responding to what they expect to happen. The difference is the whole of intimate life.

5

Memory lives in tissue.

Tissue fires faster than thought.

The Speed of Imprint

Every pattern the nervous system runs today was written by an experience it was trying to survive. The nervous system operates as a forecasting system. It scans for resemblance, not accuracy. It organizes around familiarity, not truth.

A delay in response resembles past abandonment. Distance resembles past loss. Praise resembles conditional love. Intense desire resembles past instability.

The body does not categorize these consciously; it recognizes patterns. Activation begins long before language. Your identity believes it is in control; however, your body knows better. High-functioning adults are often the most confused by this. Competence creates the illusion of regulation. Achievement creates the illusion of stability.

Professional success does not recalibrate imprint. Intellectual maturity does not update tissue memory. You can be capable and still dysregulated in intimacy. You can be confident and still collapse under desire. You can be accomplished and still react like a twelve-year-old. Insight offers awareness. Capacity offers choice. Most people possess the former. Few build the latter.

Imprint Becomes Expectation

A woman sits across from me. Calm. Articulate. Successful. She describes her relationship as secure.

"He's consistent. He's kind. He communicates."

Her voice tightens when she mentions response time.

"When he doesn't text for a few hours, something shifts."

Nothing has occurred.

No rupture.

No argument.

No betrayal.

Only time.

Her chest tightens.

Her thoughts spiral.

Her desire cools.

"What does it feel like?" I ask.

"Like I'm about to be replaced."

She tells me about being twelve.

Waiting for her father to pick her up.

He never arrived.

Absence embedded itself as prediction.

Her current partner is reliable. Her nervous system does not differentiate between memory and moment. Delay resembles abandonment. Uncertainty resembles loss. Her body responds accordingly.

Desire withdraws first.

If she anticipates being replaced, she refuses to stay open.

If she anticipates instability, she numbs hunger.

If she anticipates loss, she protects access.

She interprets the shift as a loss of attraction.

The mechanism is protection.

Imprint predicts.

Prediction triggers contraction.

Contraction alters perception.

Perception drives reaction.

The sequence completes before conscious thought can intervene.

The Identity Illusion

High-functioning adults often believe they have outthought this. They speak fluently about attachment. They can name their patterns. They understand trauma theory. Their bodies still contract. Competence disguises fragility. Polish disguises reactivity. Sexual confidence disguises instability.

Desire amplifies imprint.

Power amplifies imprint.

Intimacy amplifies imprint.

Anything that increases exposure increases prediction. Many adults cool their desire when intimacy deepens. Many adults choose partners who feel safe but flat. Many adults sabotage expansion when power increases. Their nervous system associates aliveness with risk. Boredom feels manageable. Intensity feels dangerous. Attraction destabilizes when safety is uncertain. The body protects itself by lowering emotional charge. That protection masquerades as preference.

Sovereignty Requires Capacity

Regulation is not suppression. Capacity is the ability to feel activation without surrendering to it. Capacity allows contraction without collapse, allows desire without panic, allows silence without story. Most people attempt to repair the relationship. Few build the nervous system required to sustain one; most attempt to modify circumstances. Few modify the prediction.

Your nervous system continues running its oldest predictions until you demonstrate in real time that they no longer apply. Demonstration requires presence. Presence requires regulation. Regulation requires repetition.

Without capacity, intimacy remains volatile.

Without capacity, desire remains unstable.

Without capacity, power feels threatening.

You cannot build sovereign love on a reactive foundation.

You cannot sustain polarity while outsourcing stability.

3

Chapter Three

You Don't Miss Them. You Miss the Activation.

Adrenaline feels erotic when unpredictability was your first language of love. She says she wants passion, but she means she craves the spike-the late-night text, the almost, the uncertainty, the edge. He says he wants chemistry; he means he seeks the tension of not knowing whether he is chosen. We call it spark. We call it magnetic. We call it rare. Most people chase activation, mistaking it for desire, but true intimacy is rooted in steadiness, not chaos.

You did not fall for them. You fell for ignition. The tightness. The anticipation. The ache. You could not eat. You could not sleep. You replayed every word. Adrenaline feels erotic when unpredictability was your first language of love.

If attention was inconsistent, if affection had to be earned, if connection was unstable, your body wired tension to mean intimacy. Calm does not spike. Calm softens. Softening feels empty to a system trained on volatility.

So when someone is steady, available, and present, your body does not surge. It exhales. You interpret that exhale as boredom. You say the chemistry faded. What faded was cortisol.

Intensity is easy. Polarity requires capacity.

Intensity is two dysregulated nervous systems colliding. Polarity is two regulated adults consciously choosing tension. One explodes—the other hums.

Magnetism requires presence. Most people chase explosions. Explosions feel alive. Magnetism feels exposed. Exposure requires regulation. A man once told me he had never felt passion as he did with her. "She was fire," he said. "Unpredictable. Wild. I never knew where I stood."

When she withdrew, he felt electric. When she returned, he felt chosen. When she threatened to leave, he felt alive. He mistook instability for depth.

His nervous system equated volatility with desire. The relationship ended in exhaustion. He said he missed her. What he missed was the surge.

The unavailable lover activates pursuit. The volatile partner activates control. The one who withdraws activates the performance of worthiness.

Every spike feels like desire. Until the crash. What rises fast collapses fast.

Then you say, "I lost the spark.

"You did not lose the spark. You lost the chaos your body mistook for aliveness.

Erotic maturity feels different. You can feel heat without losing yourself. You can experience charge without chasing it. You can sit in steadiness without manufacturing drama. Desire remains alive. It no longer destabilizes you. The pulse hums instead of spikes. That hum is quieter. It is also sustainable.

So ask yourself: Where are you confusing anxiety with attraction? Where does calm feel suspicious? Where does steadiness feel flat? If unpredictability were not required to feel desire, what would intimacy look like then?

You never missed them. You missed the spike.

Before you answer those questions in your mind, take them to the body first. Sit upright. Feel the weight of your hips in the chair. Take one slow breath and let the exhale be complete before you begin.

Now bring to mind someone who felt like home and chaos simultaneously. Do not analyze the relationship. Do not build a case for or against it. Let their face arrive in your imagination and notice what happens immediately in your chest. Notice what happens in the belly. Notice whether the breath shortens, the jaw tightens, or something in the throat closes slightly. That response, whatever it is, is not a memory. It is a prediction still running.

Now bring to mind someone who offered you steadiness. Someone whose presence was consistent, whose affect was regulated, whose attention did not spike and withdraw. And notice the body's response to that image. Notice if there is warmth, and notice if there is also, beneath the warmth, a faint flatness. A sense of something missing that you could not name.

That flatness is not evidence that the steady person was wrong for you.

It is evidence of what your nervous system was trained to recognize as love.

You are not looking for a conclusion here. You are looking for data. The body has been keeping the account of what its learned desire feels like. This is the moment to begin reading it.

Stay here for as long as it takes for something to become clear. Then, when you are ready, ask: What would it mean to let steadiness be enough?

4

Chapter Four

Polarity Without Collapse

The argument starts over something small. It always does.

A tone. A look. A comment that lands sharper than intended. She feels the shift first. Her body tightens. Heat rises. Words line up behind her teeth.

He feels it a second later. His chest constricts. His jaw sets. His instinct is to pull back. Two nervous systems meet.

In most relationships, this is where collapse begins.

She escalates to feel power. He withdraws to feel control. She grows louder. He grows colder. She accuses. He shuts down.

The charge spikes. Both call it passion. Both call it miscommunication. Both are outsourcing their nervous systems to each other.

Now watch what happens when the collapse does not occur:

She feels the heat rise and stays seated. Her breath slows deliberately. Her eyes remain steady.

"I'm angry," she says. "But I'm still here."

He feels the urge to withdraw. He notices it. His body wants distance. He stays.

"I'm activated," he says. "I'm not leaving."

The air thickens. There is tension. There is heat. There is no explosion.

This is polarity. Not volatility. Not domination. Not shut down. Polarity is tension held consciously. Two regulated adults choosing to remain present in charge. She does not perform her anger. He does not suppress his discomfort. Neither collapses into old imprint. The energy between them hums instead of detonating. That hum is erotic. Not because it is chaotic, but because it is contained.

Before you continue, try this:

Bring to mind a moment of conflict, real, recent, unresolved enough to still carry some charge. Do not choose the most activated memory you have. Choose something manageable. A disagreement. A moment of tension. Something that left residue.

Feel where it lives in the body right now, just from the recollection. Notice the chest. Notice the jaw. Notice whether the breath shortened when the memory arrived.

Now locate your feet. Feel them against the floor, the full weight and surface of them, the pressure of the ground beneath them; this is not a distraction from the memory. It is information you are adding to it. The body can hold both: the activation of the memory and the ground beneath the feet. Let both be true simultaneously.

Now take three slow exhales. Not the sharp exhale of someone releasing stress. The long, deliberate exhale of a body deciding to stay.

Notice what shifts in the chest. Notice if the jaw softens even slightly. Notice whether the memory still carries the same charge or whether something has begun to move in it.

This is what regulation feels like in the middle of activation. Not the absence of charge. The presence of ground beneath it. This is the practice that makes the second scene in this chapter possible. Not a technique applied in the moment of conflict, but a capacity built in moments like this one, when the body learns, repetition by repetition, that it can feel the heat and remain standing.

The next time conflict arises in real time, you will not need to remember this practice. The body will already know it.

That is how we build capacity.

Most people have only experienced polarity through dysregulation. They mistake emotional whiplash for sexual chemistry. They mistake shutdown for masculinity. They mistake escalation for feminine power. These are not character flaws; they are wounds wearing gender's clothing.

True polarity requires internal leadership. Without regulation, tension becomes a threat. With regulation, tension becomes attraction. She can express intensity without destabilizing him. He can hold steadiness without diminishing her. That dynamic creates current. Not the spike of adrenaline. The slow burn of magnetism. Two bodies in contact. Two nervous systems are steady. Charge without collapse.

That is erotic power.

Most couples never reach it. They oscillate between explosion and avoidance. They call it normal. They call it "just how we are."

Polarity does not disappear in long-term relationships. It collapses under dysregulation.

When one partner must shrink to maintain peace, attraction dies. When one partner must dominate to feel safe, intimacy erodes. Regulated polarity feels different. She remains powerful without attacking. He remains grounded without retreating. Tension exists. Safety exists alongside it. Desire grows inside that container. The argument becomes foreplay for depth. The rupture becomes a door; a door on how to stay. How to feel charge, how to hold each other in activation without fragmentation.

Power without volatility. Intensity without chaos. Desire without collapse.

That is the reclamation. Two people. Still in the room. Still in contact. The argument is unresolved. The connection is intact.

5

Chapter Five

Staying in Your Body When the Heat Rises

Desire does not disappear.

YOU leave.

You leave your body the moment intensity rises. You leave when you feel too exposed. You leave when pleasure builds too fast. You leave when conflict tightens your chest. You leave when someone looks at you too deeply.

And then you say the spark faded.

The spark did not fade.

Your capacity did.

Most people cannot stay present in high charge, and high charge is not only what happens in bed. High charge is sexual eye contact held one breath too long. It is conflict with someone you cannot afford to lose. It is devotion offered without condition. It is being wanted so completely it frightens you. It is being seen so clearly that you want to disappear. It is being held accountable by someone who stays anyway. It is being desired not for your performance but for your presence.

Charge is energy moving. And if your nervous system learned that intensity equals danger, you will shut down, escalate, or distract when the current builds. Not consciously. Somatically. The exit happens before the decision.

Erotic maturity is the ability to stay.

To feel the pulse in your belly and not manufacture distance. To feel the heat in your chest and not convert it into conflict. To feel the vulnerability rising in your throat and not swallow it into performance.

No escape. No collapse. No manipulation. No shutdown.

Just presence.

That is where polarity stabilizes. That is where magnetism deepens. That is where desire becomes something that does not need to be chased because it has somewhere safe to live.

Most people try to increase chemistry. Very few increase capacity.

Capacity is what allows pleasure to expand without tipping into anxiety. It is what allows you to hold eye contact while your heart races, without looking away. It is what allows you to hear hard truths without imploding, to receive devotion without deflecting, to be chosen without immediately testing whether the choosing will hold.

Capacity is what allows sex to be devotional instead of transactional.

Capacity is trained and not wished for. Not understood into existence, not processed in retrospect. Trained. In the body. In real time. In the moments when everything in you wants to leave.

Notice the next time your eyes want to drop during eye contact. Stay one breath longer. That breath is the practice.

The next time conflict tightens your chest, feel your feet before you speak. Not instead of speaking. Before. Let the ground remind your nervous system that you are not in danger. Then speak from that place.

The next time pleasure builds faster than feels comfortable, breathe into it rather than away from it. See what your body does when you stop evacuating sensation. See how much more of yourself becomes available when you stop managing the temperature.

The next time someone looks at you with full attention, and your instinct is to deflect with humor, with busyness, with a redirect, stay. Let yourself be seen for three seconds longer than feels easy. Notice that you survive it. Notice what opens when you do.

These are not exercises. They are experiments in remaining. Each one expands the window. Each one teaches the nervous system that intensity is not the same as threat. Each one builds the body that sovereign love requires.

When a woman can stay open in pleasure without testing, she becomes radiant. When a man can stay grounded in intensity without withdrawing, he becomes magnetic. When both can stay embodied during heat, desire compounds. Not spikes. Compounds.

These are not prescriptions. They are invitations back to what wounding interrupted.

Because most of us were not taught to stay, we were taught to manage. To perform. To exit gracefully before the feeling became too large to contain. We learned to leave our bodies so skillfully that we stopped noticing the departure.

We called the numbness maturity. We called the distance discernment. We called the shutdown selectivity. It was none of those things. It was a nervous system doing exactly what it learned to do in a world that did not know how to hold intensity with care.

You can learn to stay.

Not by forcing presence. Not by overriding the signal. Not by shaming yourself back into the room. By building, slowly, repetitively, somatically, a nervous system that no longer equates aliveness with danger.

By practicing, in small moments, the thing the large moments require. By discovering, one breath at a time, that you can feel without fracturing. That heat does not have to mean harm. That charge does not have to mean chaos. That being fully seen, does not have to mean being destroyed.

If you want desire that lasts, increase your capacity to stay. If you want polarity that does not burn out, build the body that can hold it. If you want sovereign love, learn to feel without leaving. The work is not out there. It has never been out there.

It is here.

In the body.

In the breath.

In the choice to remain.

6

Chapter Six

The Timing of Repair

The argument is not the problem.

The timing is.

Most couples do not fail because they have irreconcilable differences. They fail because they try to resolve those differences while their nervous systems are still in a state of fight-or-flight. They bring words to a conversation that first requires neurbiology. They expect language to do what only regulation can do.

And then they wonder why nothing changes.

The Body in Conflict

Before the first word lands in an argument, the body has already made a decision.

The heart rate has climbed. The chest has tightened. The peripheral vision has narrowed. Breathing has become shallow and fast. The prefrontal cortex, the part of the brain responsible for nuance, empathy, and long-term thinking, has stepped back. Something older has stepped forward.

This is sympathetic activation: fight-or-flight. The nervous system has assessed the situation and determined that a threat is present. It is doing exactly what it was designed to do.

In sympathetic activation, you are faster. You are louder. You are certain. Your arguments feel airtight. Your grievances feel irrefutable. You can access every wrong ever done to you with startling clarity and arrange them into a case so complete it feels like truth.

It is not truth.

It is threat logic, which triggers survival responses that hinder emotional regulation and prevent genuine connection. Threat logic is not designed for intimacy. It is designed for survival.

Then there is the other exit. The one that looks like calm but isn't.

Dorsal shutdown is the deeper layer of the protective response. It arrives when fight-or-flight stops feeling viable. The body goes flat. The voice goes quiet. The eyes go distant. Words become monosyllabic. Presence becomes performance. The lights are on. Nobody is home.

This is not peace. This is the nervous system pulling the emergency brake.

From the outside, it can look like maturity, like someone who doesn't escalate, who stays quiet, who doesn't make things worse. From the inside it looks like absence. The person has left the room without moving their body.

Neither state, activation nor shutdown is capable of genuine repair.

You cannot negotiate from inside a threat response. You cannot connect from inside a collapse. Trying to resolve conflict while dysregulated is not a communication problem. It is a biological problem. It is like performing surgery while the building is on fire. The fire must be addressed first.

And yet most people keep talking.

The Erotic Cost of Poor Timing

Every unresolved argument leaves something behind.

Not always consciously. Not always in words. But the body keeps the account. A conversation that ended in shutdown rather than repair leaves residue. A conflict that escalated past the point of return and never came back leaves residue. An apology offered before regulation, mechanical, performed, designed to end the discomfort rather than address the rupture, leaves residue.

Residue accumulates.

It becomes a slight tension before bed. The careful distance in the kitchen. The absence of spontaneous touch. The sex that stops happening without either person naming why. The humor that develops an edge. The tenderness that requires effort didn't used to require it.

Most couples attribute this to time. To familiarity. To the natural flattening of long-term love.

It is not time.

It is unprocessed activation living in the tissue between two people.

Because polarity cannot thrive where the nervous system feels unsafe, desire does not survive in an environment where repair consistently fails. The body that has learned to brace in the presence of its partner cannot simultaneously open to them. Protection and surrender cannot occupy the same nervous system at the same time.

When repair fails, the erotic field contracts.

When the erotic field contracts, distance becomes the default.

When distance becomes the default, both people begin to

grieve something they cannot name.

They call it losing the spark.

It was never the spark.

It was safety. And safety is repaired. Deliberately. In the body. In the moments after rupture.

Sovereignty in Conflict

A sovereign nervous system does not win arguments.

It recognizes when it can no longer have one.

This is not weakness. It is the most sophisticated form of relational intelligence available, the ability to read your own internal state with enough accuracy to know: I am no longer here. I am in threat. Whatever comes out of my mouth right now will not serve this relationship, this person, or the truth I actually want to speak.

And then to pause.

Not to avoid. Not to suppress. Not to withdraw as punishment or protection. But to pause with intention; to name the pause, to make it legible to the person across from you, and to return when the body is ready to be present again.

"I want to continue this. I am not regulated enough to do it well right now. Give me a few minutes."

That sentence is an act of sovereignty. It requires more courage than escalation. It requires more strength than shut-down. It requires a nervous system that has practiced enough to recognize its own threshold and to value the relationship more than being right in this moment.

Sovereigns do not argue in threat. They wait for coherence. Not because they are conflict-avoidant. Because they under-stand that coherence is when words finally have a chance to land.

The Three-Minute Reset

Before continuing a hard conversation, try this.

No phones. No explanation required. Simply: three minutes.

Sit facing each other or back-to-back, whichever feels more manageable in the moment. Let the eyes soften or close. Feel the feet on the floor. Breathe slowly, not the breath of performance, not the demonstrative sigh of someone making a point, but the quiet, deliberate breath of a body asking itself to return.

Do not speak. Do not process. Do not begin formulating your next point.

Just regulate.

Three minutes of shared breath does something that no amount of communication technique can replicate: it brings two nervous systems back into the same room, not into agreement. Not into resolution. Into presence. And presence is where repair becomes possible.

Notice what shifts. Notice whether the words you were about to say still feel necessary. Notice whether the tone you were carrying softens. Notice whether the person across from you begins to look less like an opponent and more like someone you chose.

Often, the argument's content has not changed. But the body's relationship to it has. And that changes everything about what gets said next, and how, and whether it lands as intended.

This is not a technique for avoiding hard conversations. It is a technique for having them. It is the difference between words fired from activation and words spoken from ground.

That difference is the whole of repair.

Why This Feels Hard

For many people, slowing down in conflict does not feel like wisdom.

It feels like losing. The urgency to speak, to be heard, to

defend, to correct the record before it solidifies, feels necessary. The pressure behind the words feels like truth trying to escape. Pausing feels like surrender. Regulation feels like suppression. Breathing feels like conceding ground that cannot be recovered.

This is not irrationality.

This is history.

For many nervous systems, urgency once meant survival. Speaking fast meant being believed. Escalating meant being taken seriously. Silence meant erasure. Stillness meant defeat.

Those adaptations were intelligent. They worked in the environments that required them. They destroy intimacy in environments that don't.

Because urgency in adulthood, urgency deployed against someone you love, in a moment that calls for presence rather than pressure, does not create safety. It creates more activation. It escalates the very threat response it is trying to resolve. Two people, each convinced that speaking faster and louder will finally produce understanding, each becoming less capable of understanding with every word.

Regulation is not suppression. It is not the performance of calm. It is not the denial of feeling.It is the decision to feel fully, and to wait until the body can carry that feeling into language without weaponizing it.

That decision is strength. It is among the most difficult things a nervous system can be asked to do, and it is learnable.

Most fights are not about their content.They are about nervous systems speaking before their bodies are ready to hear. The words are real. The grievances are real. The pain is real. But the timing, the insistence on resolution before regulation, turns real pain into ongoing harm.

When timing aligns with regulation, conflict becomes intimacy. Two people who can rupture and return, who can feel the heat of genuine disagreement and navigate back toward each other, that is not conflict avoided. That is trust built in real time. That is the body learning, repetition by repetition, that this relationship is a place it can survive being honest.

When timing ignores the body, conflict becomes erosion. Slow, cumulative, almost invisible until the day one person realizes they stopped reaching for the other, and cannot remember exactly when.

Repair is not a conversation.

It is a practice.

And, as with all practices, it begins not with the right words but with the regulated body that can finally receive them.

7

Chapter Seven

The Shadow of Power

She reaches across the table and takes his hand. "I just want you to know," she says, "that I see how hard you've been working. On yourself. On us. I feel you differently lately. I feel you here."

He smiles. It is a good smile — warm, present, the smile of someone who has done enough therapy to know how to receive.

"Thank you," he says. "That means a lot."

He squeezes her hand. He means it. And then, smoothly, without drama, without even noticing the movement, he picks up his coffee cup with his other hand and says something about the week ahead. Something about a meeting. Something that makes her laugh. She laughs. The moment passes.

What he did not do, what he could not do, what the part of him that had spent years building composure would not permit, was let it land, let her words move through the careful architecture of his self-possession and reach the place underneath where the younger version of him was still waiting to be told that he was seen.

28

He received the love correctly.

He did not receive it fully.

And she felt it, not as rejection, nothing as legible as that. She felt it as a faint distance. A glass between them that she could see through but not touch through. A warmth that stopped just short of contact.

She has felt it before. She will feel it again. She does not yet have language for what it is. He does not know it is happening. This is the shadow of power. Not cruelty. Not avoidance. Not the dramatic withdrawal of the dysregulated lover. Just a man who has learned to stand so steadily that he has forgotten how to be reached.

There is a moment when reclaiming yourself feels intoxicating. You stop chasing. You stop explaining. You stop shrinking. You hold your center. It feels electric.

But here's what almost no one tells you: Power without integration becomes armor. You say you have standards. But you're unavailable. You say you're regulated. But you're unreachable. You say you don't tolerate inconsistency. But you no longer risk intimacy. It looks like strength. It feels like control. It is often fear with better posture.

The overgiver dissolves into others. The hardened sovereign dissolves connection entirely. Both are protective. Both are reactive. One says, "I don't need you to leave." The other says: I don't need you. Neither is fully open.

Because the wound beneath the overgiver and the wound beneath the hardened sovereign are closer than either would like to admit, one learned that love required self-erasure. The other learned that self-erasure was too costly, and built a fortress instead. Both are still organizing around the original injury. Both are still, in their own way, asking the same question.

Is it safe to be here?

You can weaponize self-awareness.

You can call shutdown boundaries. You can call avoidance discernment. You can call emotional distance peace. You can call superiority sovereignty. The language is refined. The nervous system is still guarding.

And polarity dies quietly in guarded systems. Because polarity requires tension. And tension requires vulnerability. And vulnerability requires a nervous system willing to be affected, not managed, not observed from a careful distance, not held at arm's length by sophisticated analysis.

Affected.

That word is the threshold. The place where real power lives and where armor reveals itself as armor. Because armor, however well-constructed, cannot be touched. And the whole project of sovereign love is not invulnerability.

It is presence.

There is a version of power that seduces. And there is a version of power that intimidates. If people feel small around you, that is not sovereignty. If people feel they can never reach you, that is not regulation. If your calm creates distance instead of safety, that is not regulation. It is protection. Protection that learned how to speak confidently.

The difference is felt immediately in the body of the person across from you. True power creates a field in which others feel more like themselves, more seen, more steady, more capable of their own truth. Armored power creates a field in which others feel subtly insufficient. Like they are always slightly missing the mark. Like warmth is available in theory, but never quite lands. You can feel the difference. So can everyone around you.

The shadow does not announce itself. It arrives as withholding affection to regain leverage, as pulling away to feel in control. As needing to be right. As needing to be unmoved, as needing, above all, to be the one less affected.

It feels powerful.

Until you realize you have eliminated the very thing power was supposed to protect. Not weakness. Not smallness. Intimacy. And intimacy is where polarity actually lives, not in the performance of strength, not in the architecture of distance, but in the charged and vulnerable space between two people who have chosen to remain present with each other despite every instinct that says leave. You cannot access that space from behind armor. No matter how elegant the armor is.

True sovereignty is permeable. It can hold power and still soften. It can lead and still listen. It can maintain standards and still feel. It can stay when things get uncomfortable, not because discomfort is sought, but because the relationship is valued more than the relief of exit.

That is mature power, and mature power is magnetic, not because it dominates but because it dares. It dares to be seen in uncertainty. It dares to say I don't know. It dares to let someone's love land without immediately testing whether it will hold. It dares to need.

That last one is the hardest. For the person who built sovereignty out of self-sufficiency, allowing genuine need to be visible, not performed vulnerability, not strategic disclosure, but real, unglamorous, unresolved need, feels like dismantling everything they constructed.

It is not dismantling. It is completing.

Because sovereignty without the capacity for need is not freedom, it is a more sophisticated cage. And the people inside it are often the loneliest people in the room, surrounded by admiration, starved for contact.

Shadow integration is not about diminishing your power. It is not a return to the overgiver, the pleaser, the one who made themselves small to keep the peace. It is not trading one wound for another. It is about making power relational.

It is about building a self so internally coherent that you can afford to be affected, because you know you will not be destroyed by it. Because the ground is solid enough that you can let someone close without losing your footing. Because regulation is deep enough that vulnerability is no longer a threat.

That is the completion of the work this book has been building toward.

Not power for its own sake. Not sovereignty as isolation. Not regulation as distance, but power in contact. Sovereignty in relationship. Regulation in the service of genuine intimacy.

Where have you used strength to avoid being seen?

Where have you chosen control instead of connection?

Where has your power made you safer, but less intimate?

Sit with those questions in the body, not the mind. Notice where they land. Notice what tightens. Notice what, beneath the tightening, quietly wants something different.

Power that cannot risk vulnerability will always stand alone. And standing alone is not sovereignty.

It is survival.

You have already survived.

The work now is to live.

8

Chapter Eight

Devotion and Leadership

There are two capacities that sovereign love requires above all others. Not passion. Not chemistry, not compatibility, but devotion and leadership. Not as roles assigned by gender or expectation. Not as performances calibrated for attraction. But as relational capacities, ways of showing up that emerge from a regulated nervous system and a self secure enough to give without losing itself in the giving.

Most people have experienced distorted versions of both. Devotion that curdled into dependency. Leadership that hardened into control. So they approach both with suspicion, holding back their devotion in case it makes them too available, softening their leadership in case it makes them too much. This chapter is about what both look like when they are no longer distorted.

Devotion is not obsession. It is not the intensity of early attachment, the constant reach, the monitoring of response. It is not the overgiver's reflex or the anxious lover's persistence.

Devotion is consistency.

It is the choice, made repeatedly and without fanfare, to turn toward instead of away. To stay curious when defensiveness would be easier. To show up again after conflict instead of disappearing into the wound. To remain interested in the interior life of another person long after the novelty has settled into familiarity.

Devotion is regulated presence applied over time. That is why it feels safe. Not because it is dramatic, it is rarely dramatic, but because it is reliable. Because the nervous system of the person receiving it begins, slowly and then all at once, to stop bracing for withdrawal. Begins to trust the ground beneath the relationship. Begins to open in ways that intensity never permitted because intensity always carried the threat of its own ending.

Devotion does not spike. It accumulates. And what accumulates in a nervous system that has learned to trust another person's consistency is not dependency. It is the particular freedom of feeling genuinely held, the freedom that allows desire to deepen rather than ignite and exhaust itself.

Notice the quality of your presence with the people you love most.

Not the frequency, presence is not proximity. You can be in the same room as someone every day and be consistently elsewhere. You can be geographically distant and devotionally close.

Notice whether you turn toward or away when the relationship asks something difficult of you. Notice whether curiosity or defensiveness arrives first when your partner shares something uncomfortable. Notice whether you show up differently after conflict: more careful, more managed, more performed, or whether you return as yourself.

You do not need to answer these questions aloud. Let the

body answer first. Place one hand on the chest and ask: " Am I here?" Not "am I a good partner?" Not "am I trying hard enough? Simply: "Am I here, now, in this relationship, with this person?" Whatever the body says, stay with it. No judgment. No correction. Just the beginning of devotion practiced from awareness rather than reflex.

Leadership is not loud. It does not announce itself. It does not require an audience, a hierarchy, or a partner diminished by contrast.

Leadership is containment.

It is the capacity to remain grounded when emotion rises in the room, not by suppressing it or managing it from a careful distance, but by being regulated enough that the emotion can move through the field without destabilizing the structure. It is making decisions based on clarity rather than anxiety. It is initiating repair after rupture without waiting for permission or precedent. It is creating structure, a direction, a steadiness, a held container, without converting that structure into control.

When someone can hold steady while energy moves, the nervous system of the person across from them relaxes, not because they have been managed, but because they have been met by something that does not flinch. And a nervous system that is no longer bracing for the ground to shift can finally, fully, open. That opening is not weakness. It is the body's intelligent response to genuine safety. It is what becomes possible when leadership is embodied rather than performed.

Think of a moment when you held steady for someone else, when emotion was moving in the room, and you remained grounded, not through suppression but through genuine regulation- a moment when your steadiness created space rather than distance.

Feel what that was like in the body. The particular quality of being rooted while remaining open. The way the chest can be both settled and available at the same time. The way genuine, regulated presence, not performance or management, changes the field between two people.

If that memory is not readily available, that is also information. It may mean that steadiness has primarily felt like shutdown rather than leadership. That holding the field has required closing rather than rooting.

Both are worth knowing. Both are worth sitting with.

Leadership cannot be performed into existence. It is built from the inside, in moments of practice, in small repetitions of choosing ground over reaction, in the gradual discovery that you can hold something without controlling it. That discovery, made in the body, is where genuine leadership begins.

In immature dynamics, devotion looks like dependency. It clings. It monitors. It makes its presence felt through need rather than choice. It says: I am here because I cannot bear to be anywhere else.

In immature dynamics, leadership looks like control. It directs without listening. It holds the field by flattening everything that rises in it. It says: I am steady because I have made certain that nothing can move me.

Both are protective adaptations wearing the clothes of relational capacity. Both were developed in environments where genuine devotion was unreliable and genuine leadership was unsafe. Both make complete sense as responses to those environments.

And both foreclose the thing they are trying to create.

In a sovereign partnership, devotion and leadership are mutual and fluid. One may initiate. One may soften. Roles may shift with context, with season, with the particular need of a particular moment. A person who leads in one domain devotes in another. A person who softens in intimacy holds steady in conflict.

What does not shift is the underlying current.

No one is overpowering. No one is collapsing. Two adults are participating, each bringing the fullness of their regulated self into contact with the fullness of another.

Grounded devotion is rare. And because it is rare, it is profoundly attractive, not with the attraction of novelty or a spike, but with the deeper magnetism of something the nervous system has always been looking for, without knowing how to name it.

Most people oscillate. They are present and then absent. Available and then withdrawn. Warm and then distant. The oscillation is not cruelty; it is dysregulation. It is a nervous system that cannot sustain consistent presence because presence itself carries too much charge.

Few people stay steady. Few repair without ego. Few remain genuinely available after discomfort, not performing availability, not suppressing the impulse to withdraw, but actually remaining present in the aftermath of rupture and choosing to return.

That steadiness builds trust. Trust builds safety. Safety allows polarity to hum instead of explode. And in that hum, quiet, consistent, beneath the surface of daily life, desire does not fade. It deepens. It becomes the kind of desire that does not require drama to survive because it is not built on drama. It is built on the far more durable foundation of two people who have learned to trust each other's presence.

Devotion without regulation becomes clingy. Leadership

without humility becomes rigid. These are the shadow versions, the immature expressions that collapse the very dynamic they are reaching for. But devotion with self-possession becomes magnetic. Not because it withholds, the magnetism of self-possession is not the magnetism of unavailability. It is the magnetism of someone who is fully here, fully present, fully choosing, and whose choice carries weight precisely because it is not compulsive. Because they could leave. Because they have enough ground to stand on to say that staying is a genuine decision rather than a fearful reflex.

Leadership with emotional availability becomes secure. And secure is erotic in ways adrenaline never was.

Because secure does not spike. It builds. It builds across conversations and conflicts and repairs and ordinary mornings. It builds in the moments that do not look like intimacy, the consistency, the small returns, the willingness to be uncomfortable in service of something real. And what it builds is not the temporary heat of activation but the sustainable warmth of a nervous system that has finally, deeply, learned that it is safe to be here.

That warmth is the erotic field of long-term sovereign love.

A grounded person does not lead to dominate. They lead to create coherence, to hold the field steady enough that both people can move freely within it. Not because one person is more capable or more valuable, but because steadiness is a gift offered to the relationship rather than a power asserted over a partner.

A grounded person does not devote to dissolve. They devote from choice, from the fullness of a self that has enough internal coherence to turn toward another without losing its own direction. Not because they need the devotion to mean something about their worth, but because the act of consistent, chosen orientation toward someone you love is one of the most sovereign things a human being can do. Both can stand alone.

Both choose to stand together.

That is polarity matured. Not theatrical. Not reactive. Not organized around the nervous system's oldest fears.

Stable. Chosen. Alive.

After shadow comes relief, not the relief of resolution, sovereign love does not resolve into stillness. It remains alive, charged, in motion. But after the work of integration, after the honest confrontation with armor and with the wounds beneath it, something exhales.

Devotion no longer feels risky because the self giving it is not disappearing in the giving. Because the ground is solid enough that turning toward another does not mean losing your own direction. Because you have built, through the work of the previous chapters, the internal coherence that makes sustained orientation toward another person possible without collapse.

Leadership no longer feels threatening, because it is no longer organized around dominance or the suppression of what rises. It has been separated from the control it once required for safety, and it can now hold a field through presence rather than force.

What remains, when distortion falls away, is something quieter than passion and more durable than chemistry. Two people. Steady. Choosing. Present. Not because they have to be. Because they have built the capacity to stay, and they know now, in the body, not just the mind, what that capacity makes possible.

9

Chapter Nine

Sovereign Love

Sovereign love is not loud. It does not announce itself with urgency or arrive in the fever of pursuit. It does not spike and crash, does not beg or chase, does not organize itself around the terror of loss or the hunger for proof. It does not need to be the most intense thing you have ever felt to be real. It stands.

Two regulated nervous systems meeting in genuine contact. Two adults choosing, not from scarcity, not from fear, not from the ancient wound that says this is the only one who will ever make you feel this way — but from the fullness of selves that have done the work of becoming whole enough to choose freely. Two bodies that can hold heat without leaving, can feel the charge without converting it into chaos, can stay present in the current without being swept away by it.

This is not the electricity of chaos. It is the current of coherence.

And coherence, in a world organized around activation, is the most radical and powerful thing two people can build together.

Sovereign love feels different in the body.

Not immediately recognizable, not at first, because the body that has been trained on urgency will initially read steadiness as flatness. Will scan for the familiar spike and, not finding it, conclude that something is missing. This is the nervous system doing what nervous systems do: assessing resemblance, running the old prediction, reaching for the known shape of love even when that shape was never safe.

But stay. Stay long enough for the body to learn a new pattern. Stay long enough to discover what it feels like when your breath does not tighten in their presence, when your chest stays open instead of braced. When your spine stays upright because you are not contorting yourself to maintain connection or managing yourself to avoid rupture.

Notice the absence of urgency. Then notice what is present in its place.

Choice. Quiet, uncoerced, arising from alignment rather than anxiety. The experience of wanting without needing. Of being drawn toward someone not because they activate your oldest wound but because they meet your actual self, the self that exists beneath the performance, beneath the protection, beneath the years of adaptive survival.

That is power. Not the power of control or pursuit or the upper hand in the dynamic. The power of a person who is no longer driven by abandonment, no longer propelled by adrenaline, no longer organizing their intimate life around the need to prove something to someone who isn't in the room anymore, driven by alignment.

Before the final pages of this book, before the words that close the arc, come into the body for a moment. Sit the way a person sits who is not waiting for anything. Upright without rigidity.

Present without performance. Feel the full weight of yourself in the chair, in the room, in this moment.

Take three breaths, not therapeutic, not demonstrative. Simply the breath of a body that has been traveling and has arrived somewhere.

Now let the journey of this book move through you, not as a review of concepts, not as an inventory of what you have learned. As sensation. As the felt residue of nine chapters that have been asking the same thing in different registers: come home to yourself. Stop outsourcing what only you can build. Feel what is actually here.

Notice what has shifted since the first page. Not in the mind, in the body. Is the chest slightly more open than it was? Is the jaw slightly less held? Is there a quality of recognition, not of information but of self, that was not as available when you began?

If so, that is not the book's achievement. It is yours. The book only named what the body already knew and had not yet been given language for.

Now bring to mind the love you want. Not its specific form, not the face, not the circumstances, not the relationship structure. The felt quality of it. What it would feel like in the chest to be in sovereign love. To be chosen from wholeness. To choose from wholeness. To feel the current of genuine polarity, steady, alive, uncoerced.

Let that felt sense be real in the body for a moment. Not as fantasy. As a nervous system learning the shape of what it is building toward.

This is not manifestation. It is orientation.

The nervous system moves toward what it can recognize as safe. By building the felt sense of sovereign love in the body, even briefly, even imperfectly, even as a practice rather than a reality, you are teaching the system what to recognize when it arrives. Stay here for as long as the body wants. Then, when you are ready, turn the page.

That shift, from fear to alignment as the organizing principle of love, is the entire journey of this book made real in the body. There is something transcendent about this kind of love. Not transcendent in the way that word is often used, not as an escape from the ordinary, not as spiritual performance or the aesthetics of awakening. Transcendent in the most literal and biological sense: it breaks lineage.

You are no longer reenacting what shaped you and no longer casting the familiar players in the familiar roles and running the familiar sequence toward the familiar ending, and no longer seeking in an adult relationship the resolution of a childhood wound that no adult relationship was ever designed to provide.

You are authoring something new. That is not a small thing. It is, in fact, among the most difficult things a human nervous system can be asked to do: to stop running the prediction written in the earliest years of life, in the earliest experiences of love and its failures, and to build in its place something with no prior template. Something the body does not yet fully recognize as safe because it has never fully encountered it before.

And yet when two people meet from wholeness rather than hunger, when neither is seeking completion, when both are bringing a self that has done the work of integration, the charge between them is different in quality from anything the old pattern produced. Not frantic. Not organized around the fear of loss. Not dependent on uncertainty for its heat.

It hums.

Steadily. Sustainably. With the particular depth that only

becomes available when two people are no longer using each other to regulate what they have not yet learned to regulate in themselves.

Sovereign love does not eliminate tension. This is important. The work of this book is not the work of arriving at some frictionless state where conflict ceases, and desire runs smooth, and nothing difficult ever surfaces between two people. That is not love matured. That is love sedated.

Conflict still happens. Desire still fluctuates. Life still moves and disrupts and asks more than either person expected. The nervous system still gets activated. The old imprints still surface occasionally, still reach for the familiar shape of the wound.

But nothing collapses the center. Because the internal state is no longer outsourced. Because the ground has been built repeatedly, somatically, through practices, shadow work, devotion, and regulation, and the ground holds even when the surface moves. Because both people have developed enough capacity to feel activation without becoming it, to feel the pull of the old pattern without surrendering to it, to return to themselves and to each other after rupture without requiring the rupture to be erased.

When two people refuse to outsource their center, love becomes stable without becoming stagnant. Stable because the foundation is solid. Not stagnant because the current between two embodied, growing, choosing people never stops moving.

That is rare. Most people never find it, not because it is unavailable, but because it requires something that cannot be found. It can only be built.

There is transcendence in this. Not because it is perfect. Because it is conscious, you feel yourself choosing. Not falling, not being swept, not dissolving into someone else's gravity.

Choosing, with your eyes open, with your history visible to you, with your patterns named and your shadows integrated, and your nervous system regulated enough to be present for the decision.

You feel yourself staying. Not because you cannot leave. Because you have built the capacity to remain in the discomfort of genuine intimacy without converting that discomfort into an exit. Because staying has become an act of sovereignty rather than a failure of self-respect.

You feel yourself leading and softening without losing shape, devoting without disappearing, and standing on your own ground while turning fully toward another person. Holding the tension of genuine polarity, the charge of two differentiated selves in genuine contact, without collapsing it into merger or distance.

You feel yourself whole. And from wholeness, intimacy expands rather than consumes. Instead of the slow erosion of self that characterizes love organized around fear, there is growth, the particular expansion that happens when two people are secure enough in themselves to be genuinely changed by each other. To let the other's reality land. To be moved without being destabilized. To discover, in the safety of sovereign love, dimensions of themselves that the defended self never had access to.

Most people never experience this. Not because it is reserved for the exceptional, the enlightened, or the undamaged. Because it requires maturity, and maturity is not given. It is earned through the unglamorous, repetitive, often uncomfortable work of building a self that can sustain what love actually asks of us.

It requires nervous system literacy. The ability to read your own internal state with enough accuracy to know when you are present and when you have left, when you are responding to what is actually here, and when you are running a prediction built from something that is long gone.

It requires shadow integration. The willingness to look clearly at the ways you have used strength to avoid being seen, used distance to feel safe, and used the language of growth to protect the part of you that is still organizing around the original wound.

It requires the courage to feel without fleeing. To stay in the body when the charge rises. To let devotion be real, leadership be humble, desire be sustainable, and love be something other than the emergency it once was.

It requires sovereignty.

And once you experience it, once the body learns what it feels like to be in genuine contact with another person from a place of genuine wholeness, something shifts that cannot be unshifted. Chaos loses its seduction. Intensity loses its glamour. Drama loses the particular pull it had when it was the only available proof that something real was happening.

Because you have tasted something steadier; and steadiness, when it is fully embodied, when it is not the flatness of shutdown or the performance of calm but the genuine, rooted, alive steadiness of a regulated nervous system in sovereign contact with another, is electric in a way chaos never was. Because it is real.

Sovereign love is not something you find. You do not stumble into it. You do not attract it by becoming more desirable or more healed or more aligned with some external standard of readiness. You do not wait for the right person to make it possible. You become capable of it.

Through the work. Through the practice, through the repetition of small acts of regulation and presence and repair and return. Through shadow work, somatic literacy, and the willingness to feel without fleeing through the gradual, unglamorous, irreversible process of building a self that can sustain what love actually requires.

And when you become capable of it, when the body finally knows, not just the mind but the body, in the tissue and the breath and the steadiness of a chest that no longer braces when someone comes close, everything changes about the questions you bring to love.

You stop asking: will this last? That question belongs to fear. To the nervous system still running the oldest prediction, still scanning for the familiar ending, still organizing the present around the wound of the past.

You begin asking: Can we build? And building, choosing each other not once in the fever of early attachment but again and again, in the ordinary and the difficult and the expansive moments of a shared life, from coherence instead of fear, from wholeness instead of hunger, from the sovereign ground of two people who have done the work and know what they are capable of, is the most powerful act of intimacy there is.

Not because it is easy. Because it is chosen. Every time.

This is where the arc completes. Not with arrival, sovereign love is not a destination but a practice, not a state achieved but a capacity exercised, not a place you reach but a way you move through the world and toward the people you choose.

But with orientation. With a body that knows the difference between activation and desire, between armor and strength, between the spike of adrenaline and the hum of coherence. With a nervous system that has been trained, slowly, repetitively, in the body, to recognize genuine safety and to open toward it rather than brace against it.

Internal state. Prediction and imprint. The seduction of activation. The shadow of power. Embodied presence. The timing of repair. Devotion and leadership. And now this.

Sovereign love.

Not loud. Not urgent. Not organized around the fear of its own ending.

Standing.

Chosen.

Alive.

10

Epilogue

Close this book.

Feel your body.

Not your thoughts about it. Not your inspiration. Not your agreement.

Your body.

Are you upright? Are you breathing fully? Are your shoulders forward or open?

Sovereignty is not a concept. It is posture. It is breath. It is how you sit when no one is watching.

Here is your first action.

For the next seven days, do not speak in conflict until your body is regulated. Pause. Feel your feet. Slow your breath. Then respond. Not react.

If you cannot regulate, you do not engage.

That is leadership.

Second.

Notice where you still outsource your internal state. When

someone is distant, do you spiral? When someone is disappointed, do you collapse? When someone praises you, do you inflate?

Catch it. Bring yourself back.

Your nervous system is yours to lead.

Third.

Increase your charge capacity. When someone looks at you deeply, stay. When pleasure builds, breathe. When conflict tightens your chest, do not flee.

Ten seconds longer than before.

That is embodiment.

Fourth.

Audit your power. Where are you using strength to avoid vulnerability? Where are you withholding to feel safe? Where are you calling detachment maturity?

See it. Integrate it.

So your power becomes relational rather than protective.

Finally.

Choose differently. Not once. Repeatedly.

Choose steadiness over chaos. Choose coherence over chemistry spikes. Choose repair over righteousness. Choose devotion from strength. Choose leadership without dominance.

Choose sovereign love.

Not because it is easier.

Because it is higher.

You are not waiting to find someone who can meet you.

You are becoming someone who can meet.

And when two sovereign nervous systems meet, love does not explode.

It builds.

Now go build it.

About the Author

About the Author

Charon is a somatic trauma practitioner, sex therapist, relationship coach, and spiritual mentor whose work lives at the intersection of the nervous system and the erotic life.

For two decades, Charon has guided individuals and couples through the terrain that most therapeutic approaches leave unnamed, the place where attachment wounds meet desire, where the body's intelligence exceeds the mind's understanding, and where genuine intimacy requires more than communication skills or willpower. Drawing on somatic experiencing, Imago therapy, polyvagal theory, shadow work, and sacred sexuality, Charon works with the whole person: the body that remembers, the nervous system that predicts, and the spirit that reaches toward something larger than survival.

Charon's approach is trauma-informed without being clinical, spiritually grounded without being abstract, and erotically honest without being reductive. Her approach is built on a single foundational belief: that the capacity for sovereign love, love that is chosen from wholeness rather than driven by fear, is not a personality trait. It is a nervous system capacity.

And it can be built.

In addition to private practice and group containers, Charon teaches through Connected and Conscious, a community for relational maturity and nervous system regulation, and Embodied

Tantra, a trauma-informed somatic container exploring erotic presence, polarity, and co-regulation. Charon is also a trained Compassionate Inquiry practitioner and a contributor to the Compassionate Inquiry blog, founded by Dr. Gabor Maté.

A former in-house narrator for Dreamscape Media, one of the leading audiobook publishers in North America, Charon brings the same embodied presence to the spoken word as to the page.

Sovereign in Love is Charon's first book.

holisticharon.com

About the Author

You can connect with me on:
- https://holisticharon.com/https://holisticharon.com
- https://www.facebook.com/charon.normandwidmer
- https://www.instagram.com/relational_depth
- https://gardenmassage64.substack.com
- https://www.patreon.com/c/RelationalFireStarter

www.ingramcontent.com/pod-product-compliance
Lightning Source LLC
Chambersburg PA
CBHW041647150726
48005CB00015BB/2512